TOWNSHIP OF UNION
FREE PUBLIC LIBRARY

Sunburn

TOWNSHIP OF UNION
FREE PUBLIC LIBRARY

By Sharon Gordon

Consultants

Nanci R. Vargus, Ed.D.
Primary Multiage Teacher
Decatur Township Schools, Indianapolis, Indiana

Jayne L. Waddell, R.N., M.A., L.P.C.
School Nurse, Health Educator, Lic. Professional Counselor

Children's Press®
A Division of Scholastic Inc.
New York   Toronto   London   Auckland   Sydney
Mexico City   New Delhi   Hong Kong
Danbury, Connecticut

Designer: Herman Adler Design
Photo Researcher: Caroline Anderson
The photo on the cover shows a child with a sunburn.

Library of Congress Cataloging-in-Publication Data

Gordon, Sharon.
   Sunburn / by Sharon Gordon; consultants Nanci R. Vargus...[et al.].
      p. cm. — (Rookie read-about health)
   Includes index.
   Summary: Explains what sunburn is, how it is treated, and how it
can be prevented.
   ISBN 0-516-22569-3 (lib. bdg.)   0-516-26873-2 (pbk.)
   1. Sunburn—Juvenile literature. [1. Sunburn.] I. Title. II. Series.
RL248.G67   2002
616.5—dc21   2001002692

JE
GOR
C. 1

$14.25

©2002 Children's Press®
A Division of Scholastic Inc.
All rights reserved. Published simultaneously in Canada.
Printed in the United States of America.

SCHOLASTIC and associated designs are trademarks and/or registered
trademarks of Scholastic Inc. CHILDREN'S PRESS and ROOKIE
READ-ABOUT and all associated designs are trademarks and/or
registered trademarks of Grolier Publishing Company, Inc.
1 2 3 4 5 6 7 8 9 10 R 11 10 09 08 07 06 05 04 03 02

What a beautiful day!

The Sun is shining brightly.

You can go to the beach!
It is fun to swim and play
all day.

The warm sun feels good *on* your skin. But it is not good *for* your skin.

You can get a sunburn
from too much sun.

In the winter, the Sun is low in the sky. Its rays are weak.

It is hard to get a sunburn while making a snowman!

In the summer, the Sun is high in the sky. Now the Sun's rays are very strong.

It might only take a few minutes to get a burn on a hot summer day. But it might be hours before you can see the burn.

Then it is too late!

14

You will have a painful sunburn. Your skin will start to get red. It will feel tight.

Try putting a cool towel on your hot sunburn.

Special lotions can also help take the pain away.

A very bad sunburn is called sun poisoning.

You might feel sick. You might get a headache.

19

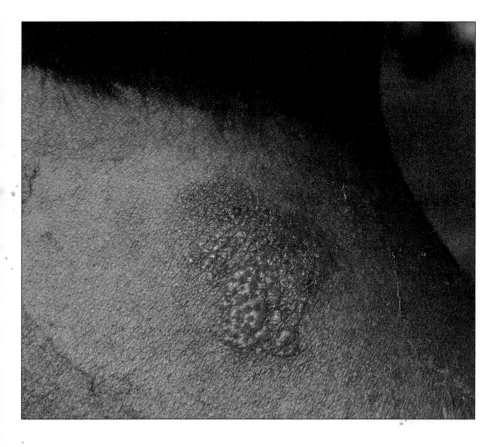

20

Your skin might blister,
just like with other types
of burns. See your doctor
if you think you have
sun poisoning.

People with light-colored
skin must be very careful.
They can burn easily.

But everyone needs to be careful in the sun. Too much sun can cause skin cancer.

Always take care of
your skin in the sun.
Use sunscreen lotion
to protect your skin.

Sit under an umbrella
at the beach.

Light-colored clothes will
keep you cool. They also
keep the Sun's rays off
your skin.

Sunglasses will protect
your eyes.

And don't forget the hat!

Words You Know

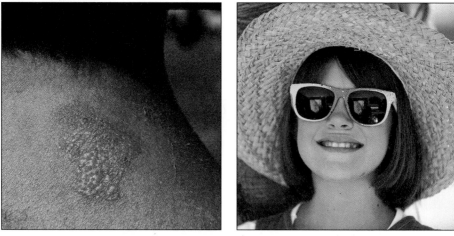

blisters

hat

lotion

sunburn

sunglasses

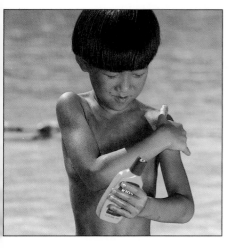

sunscreen

umbrella

31

Index

About the Author

Sharon Gordon is a writer living in Midland Park, New Jersey. She and her husband have three school-aged children and a spoiled pooch. Together they enjoy visiting the Outer Banks of North Carolina as often as possible.

Photo Credits

Photographs © 2002: Corbis-Bettmann/Tim Kiusalaas: 3; Custom Medical Stock Photo: 20, 30 top left; Photo Researchers, NY: 17, 30 bottom left (Mark Clarke/SPL), 14, 30 bottom right (Ray Ellis/SS); PhotoEdit: 4 (Bachmann), 13 (Myrleen Cate), 22 (Myrleen Ferguson), 19 (Spencer Grant), 6 (F. Martinez), 5 (Michael Newman), 27, 31 top (Frank Siteman), 25, 31 bottom right (D. Young-Wolff); Stone/Getty Images: 9 (Lori Adamski Peek), 26 (Peter Correz); Superstock, Inc.: cover; The Image Works: 24, 31 bottom left (B. Daemmrich), 23 (Winter); Visuals Unlimited: 7 (D. Cavagnaro), 10 (Roger Cole), 29, 30 top right (Cheyenne Rouse).

AAY - 6322

FREE PUBLIC LIBRARY UNION, NEW JERSEY

3 9549 00306 4087

TOWNSHIP OF UNION
FREE PUBLIC LIBRARY